The Ultimate Guide to Infinix Note 40

Unbox, Explore, and Master Your Device

Paulson Witt

All rights reserved.

Without limiting the rights under copyright reserved above, no part of this publication may be reproduced, stored in or introduced into a database and retrieval system, or transmitted in any form or by any means (electronic, mechanical, photocopying, recording, or otherwise) without the prior written permission of both the owner of the copyright and the publishers mentioned above.

Copyright©2024 Paulson Witt

Disclaimer

The author of this book has nothing but good intentions, aiming to deliver valuable and useful information. Please note that certain images and text in this book were gathered from reliable sources and were not originally created by the author. However, rest assured that everything has been carefully examined and included with the reader's or user's benefit in mind. The main focus is on making this content as helpful as possible. Your understanding is greatly appreciated.

Table Contents

GETTING STARTED 8

    Chapter 1: Unboxing and Setting Up Your Phone 8

        1.1 Introducing 8

        1.2 Package Contents 9

        1.3 Inserting the SIM Card and microSD Card 12

        1.4 Connecting to Wi-Fi 13

        1.5 Creating a User Account 13

        1.6 Transferring Data 14

    Chapter 2: Getting to Know Your Phone 16

        2.1 Physical Layout 16

            2.1.1 Buttons and Ports 16

            2.1.2 Camera Layout 18

            2.1.3 Fingerprint Sensor 18

        2.2 Home Screen and App Drawer 19

            2.2.1 Navigating the Home Screen 19

            2.2.2 Adding, Removing, and Organizing Apps 19

            2.2.3 Accessing the App Drawer 20

        2.3 Notifications Panel 20

            2.3.1 Accessing Notifications 20

            2.3.2 Clearing Notifications 21

            2.3.3 Customizing Notification Settings 21

        2.4 Quick Settings Panel 21

    ESSENTIAL FEATURES 23

Chapter 3: Making and Receiving Calls 23

3.1 Using the Dial Pad 23

3.2 Making Calls 24

3.3 Receiving Calls 24

3.4 Call History 25

3.5 Voicemail and Call Forwarding 26

Chapter 4: Text Messaging (SMS/MMS) 28

    4.1 Sending and Receiving Text Messages 28

4.2 Adding Attachments (Photos, Videos, etc.) 29

4.3 Managing Conversations 30

4.4 Customizing Message Settings 31

4.5 Using RCS (Rich Communication Services) 33

4.6 Group Messaging 34

Chapter 5: Managing Contacts 36

    5.1 Adding and Editing Contacts 36

    5.2 Creating Groups 38

    5.3 Searching for Contacts 39

    5.4 Syncing Contacts 39

    5.5 Merging Duplicate Contacts 41

    5.6 Deleting Contacts 43

    5.7 Contact Backup and Restore 43

Chapter 6: Capturing Photos and Videos 45

    6.1 Taking Photos in Auto Mode 45

    6.2 Using Different Camera Modes 47

    6.3 Recording Videos 49

6.4 Using Flash, Zoom, and HDR 50

6.5 Advanced Camera Settings 52

6.6 Customizing Camera Settings 53

6.7 Reviewing and Editing Photos and Videos 54

Chapter 7: Exploring Advanced Camera Features 56

7.1 Pro Mode for Manual Controls 56

7.2 Using the Macro Lens 58

7.3 Slow-Motion Recording 59

7.4 AI Photography Made Easy: Enhance Your Photos with Intelligence 60

7.5 Advanced Camera Settings and Customization 61

7.6 Reviewing and Editing Photos and Videos 63

Chapter 8: Camera Settings and Customization 65

8.1 Adjusting Photo and Video Resolution 65

8.2 Customizing Image Quality 67

8.3 White Balance and Exposure Controls 67

8.4 Using HDR (High Dynamic Range) 69

8.5 Focus and Depth of Field 70

8.6 Flash Settings 71

8.7 Image Stabilization 72

8.8 Customizing Camera Shortcuts 73

8.9 Reviewing and Managing Captured Media 74

8.10 Backing Up Photos and Videos 75

Maximizing Functionality 77

Chapter 9: Fingerprint Unlock and Facial Recognition 77

9.1 Setting Up Fingerprint Unlock 77

9.2 Setting Up Facial Recognition 79

9.3 Enhancing Security with Biometric Data....................81

9.4 Troubleshooting Biometric Issues................................82

Chapter 10: Connecting to Wi-Fi and Sharing Your Connection..86

10.1 Connecting to Wi-Fi Networks 86

10.2 Sharing Your Wi-Fi Connection 89

10.3 Advanced Wi-Fi Settings 91

10.4 Troubleshooting Wi-Fi Issues 93

Chapter 11: Pairing with Bluetooth Devices 96

11.1 Connecting to Bluetooth Headphones or Speakers 96

11.2 Transferring Files via Bluetooth 99

11.3 Managing Bluetooth Connections 101

11.4 Troubleshooting Bluetooth Issues 102

Chapter 12: Optimizing Battery Life 105

12.1 Understanding Battery Usage.................................105

12.2 Enabling Battery-Saving Features..........................107

12.3 Charging Your Phone...108

XOS CUSTOMIZATION 112

Chapter 13: Personalizing Your XOS Experience 112

13.1 Changing Themes and Wallpapers..........................112

13.2 Customizing Ringtones and Notifications..............114

13.3 Adjusting Launcher Settings 115

Chapter 14: Exploring Unique XOS Features 120

14.1 Using the Folax Voice Assistant 120
14.2 Enabling Lightning Multi-Window.........................122
Glossary of Phone Lingo 128
CONCLUSION...136
APPENDICES 140
  Unveiling the Specs: A Deep Dive into the Infinix Note 40 140
  Taming The Troubles: Troubleshooting Guide For Common Issues 144
  Frequently Asked Questions (FAQ)......................................148

GETTING STARTED

Chapter 1: Unboxing and Setting Up Your Phone

1.1 Introducing

Innovation knows no bounds; it evolves daily, transforming our world with each technological leap. Welcome to this dynamic era where technology reigns supreme. Today, we're diving into the remarkable realm of the Infinix Note 40. Although this marvel arrived with its siblings, our focus here is solely on the Note 40—a device that redefines excellence and promises an unparalleled user experience.

If you are someone who craves the best in tech for an extraordinary experience, the Infinix Note 40 is your perfect match. This guide will be your comprehensive companion, leading you from the excitement of unboxing to mastering every feature and function. Get ready to explore, discover, and maximize the potential of your Infinix Note 40, as we embark on this exciting journey together.

Just before diving in, the Infinix Note 40 comes with a lot of amazing features. It supports both direct and wireless charging. Another incredible feature is reverse charging, allowing you to charge another phone by placing it on the back of your Note 40. It's amazing, right? Now let's begin!

1.2 Package Contents

Before diving into the setup, let's take a look at what's inside the box. Inside, we have two packages: the first contains the MagPad Wireless Charger, while the second includes your device and its accessories.

- **Infinix Note 40 handset**: *Your brand-new smartphone.*

- **USB-C charging cable**: *For charging and data transfer.*

- **45-Watt Power adapter**: *To plug your charging cable into a power source.*

- **SIM ejector tool**: *A small pin-like tool used to open the SIM card tray.*

- **Quick start guide**: *Basic instructions to help you get started.*

- **MagPad Wireless Charger:** *For charging your phone, it has a magnet that helps securely hold it to the back of your phone, preventing it from falling off.*

- **Other Items:** *MagPad Phone Case, USB Type C headset, stickers, Warrant Card (Maybe Optional and Depending on your location), Screen Protector (Maybe Optional or already fix to your screen)*

1.3 Inserting the SIM Card and microSD Card

To start using your Infinix Note 40, you'll need to insert your SIM card and, if desired, a microSD card for additional storage:

- **Locate the SIM tray**: The SIM tray is found at the bottom close to your charging port.

- **Use the SIM ejector tool**: Insert the tool into the small hole next to the tray to eject it.

- **Place your SIM card and microSD card**: The tray will have designated slots for the Nano SIM card and the microSD card. Ensure the cards are placed correctly, with the metal contacts facing down.

- **Reinsert the tray**: Gently push the tray back into the device until it clicks into place.

1.4 Connecting to Wi-Fi

Once your SIM card is in place, connect your phone to a Wi-Fi network to complete the setup process:

- **Open the Settings app**: Tap the Settings icon on your home screen or app drawer.

- **Tap on Wi-Fi**: This will open the Wi-Fi settings menu.

- **Select your network**: Choose your Wi-Fi network from the list of available networks.

- **Enter the network password**: If required, type in your Wi-Fi password and tap Connect.

- **Confirm connection**: Once connected, you should see the Wi-Fi icon appear in the status bar at the top of the screen.

1.5 Creating a User Account

To access all features and services, you'll need to create or sign in to a user account:

- **Follow on-screen instructions**: During the initial setup, your phone will prompt you to sign in to a Google account.

- **Sign in to your Google account**: Enter your Google email and password. If you don't have a Google account, tap on 'Create account' and follow the instructions to set one up.

- **Sync your account**: After signing in, you'll have the option to sync your Google account with various services like Gmail, Google Photos, and Google Drive.

1.6 Transferring Data

If you consider transferring your data from the old phone to the new phone, here you go:

- **Use the Phone Clone app**: Install the Phone Clone app from the Google Play Store on both your old and new phones.

- **Follow the app's instructions**: Open the app on both devices and follow the prompts to connect them. This usually involves scanning a QR code displayed on your new phone with your old phone.

- **Select the data to transfer**: Choose the types of data you want to transfer, such as contacts, photos, messages, and apps.

- **Begin the transfer**: Start the transfer process and wait for it to complete. This may take some time depending on the amount of data being transferred.

Chapter 2: Getting to Know Your Phone

2.1 Physical Layout

2.1.1 Buttons and Ports

- **Power Button**: Located on the right side of the phone, this button is used to turn the phone on and off and to lock and unlock the screen. Press and hold it to access the power menu, which includes options for restarting or powering off the device.

- **Volume Buttons**: Also on the right side, these buttons are used to adjust the volume level. The upper button increases the volume, while the lower button decreases it.

- **SIM Card Tray**: Found at the bottom of the phone close to charging port, this tray holds the SIM card and microSD card. Use the SIM ejector tool to open it.

- **USB-C Port**: Located at the bottom of the device, this port is used for charging and data transfer. It also supports USB On-The-Go (OTG) for connecting peripherals like USB drives.

- **Dual Speaker**: Also at the bottom, next to the USB-C port, is the main speaker for audio output.

- **Microphone**: Located at both the bottom and top of the phone, the microphones are used for calls and voice recording.

- **IR Blaster**: Found at the top of the device, the IR blaster can be used to control compatible appliances like TVs and air conditioners.

- **Fingerprint Sensor**: Integrated into the display, this sensor allows you to unlock your phone securely with your fingerprint.

2.1.2 Camera Layout

- **Rear Cameras**: The Infinix Note 40 features a triple camera setup on the back, including:

  - 108 MP main camera

  - 2 MP depth sensor

  - Quad-LED flash

- **Front Camera**: The punch-hole design houses a 32 MP front camera for selfies and video calls.

2.1.3 Fingerprint Sensor

- **Location**: The fingerprint sensor is embedded under the display (that is in-display fingerprint).

- **Setup**: To set up fingerprint recognition, go to *Settings > Security > Fingerprint*, and follow the prompts to add your fingerprint.

2.2 Home Screen and App Drawer

2.2.1 Navigating the Home Screen

- **Home Screen**: This is the main screen you see when you unlock your phone. It displays app icons, widgets, and shortcuts.

- **Gestures**: Swipe up from the bottom to access the app drawer, swipe down from the top for notifications, and swipe left or right to navigate between home screen panels.

- **Dock**: The bottom row of the home screen typically contains your most-used apps.

2.2.2 Adding, Removing, and Organizing Apps

- **Adding Apps**: Tap and hold an app icon from the app drawer, then drag it to the home screen.

- **Removing Apps**: Tap and hold an app icon on the home screen, then drag it to the 'Remove' option that appears at the top.

- **Organizing Apps**: Drag app icons to move them around or create folders by dragging one app onto another.

2.2.3 Accessing the App Drawer

- **Opening the App Drawer**: Swipe up from the bottom of the home screen to open the app drawer.

- **Searching for Apps**: Use the search bar at the top of the app drawer to quickly find apps.

2.3 Notifications Panel

2.3.1 Accessing Notifications

- **Swipe Down**: Swipe down from the top of the screen to access the notifications panel. This panel shows recent notifications and alerts from apps.

- **Quick Access**: Tap on a notification to open the corresponding app or perform a quick action directly from the panel.

2.3.2 Clearing Notifications

- **Clear Individual Notifications**: Swipe a notification left or right to dismiss it.

- **Clear All Notifications**: *Tap the 'Clear All' button at the bottom of the notifications panel to dismiss all notifications at once.*

2.3.3 Customizing Notification Settings

- **Settings Menu**: *Go to Settings > Notifications to customize how and when you receive notifications.*

- **Per-App Settings**: Adjust notification preferences for individual apps, including sound, vibration, and priority.

2.4 Quick Settings Panel

- **Accessing Quick Settings**: Swipe down twice from the top of the screen or swipe down once with two fingers to open the quick settings panel.

- **Toggles and Shortcuts**: This panel includes toggles for Wi-Fi, Bluetooth, Do Not Disturb, and other frequently used settings.

- **Customization**: Tap the pencil icon to edit the quick settings panel. You can add, remove, and rearrange toggles to suit your preferences.

ESSENTIAL FEATURES

Chapter 3: Making and Receiving Calls

3.1 Using the Dial Pad

- **Opening the Dial Pad**: Tap the phone icon on your home screen or in the app drawer to open the Phone app. The dial pad will be displayed by default.

- **Dialing a Number**: Enter the phone number you wish to call using the numeric keypad. As you type, the phone may suggest contacts from your address book that match the entered digits.

- **Making the Call**: After entering the number, tap the green call button to place the call.

- **Accessing Recent Calls**: Tap the "Recents" tab at the bottom of the screen to view your call history. You can tap any entry to call back.

3.2 Making Calls

- **Contacts App**: Open the Contacts app, scroll through your list, and tap the contact you wish to call. Tap the phone icon next to their number to place the call.

- **Call History**: In the Phone app's Recents tab, tap any recent call entry to redial the number.

- **Voice Commands**: You can use Google Assistant to make a call by saying, "Hey Google, call [contact name]."

3.3 Receiving Calls

- **Incoming Call Screen**: When you receive a call, your screen will show the caller's name (if saved in your contacts) and phone number.

- **Answering a Call**: Swipe the green answer icon to the right or up (as the case maybe) to answer the call.

- **Rejecting a Call**: Swipe the red decline icon to the left to reject the call. You can also reject with a message by swiping up and selecting a predefined message or writing a custom one.

- **Silencing a Call**: Press the volume down button to silence an incoming call without rejecting it.

3.4 Call History

- **Viewing Call History**: Open the Phone app and tap the "*Recents*" tab to view a log of your recent calls.

- **Details and Actions**: Tap an entry to see details such as call duration and the time of the call. You can also call back, send a message, or add the number to your contacts from this screen.

- **Clearing Call History**: To delete individual call entries, tap and hold on an entry and select

"*Delete*." To clear all call history, tap the three-dot menu in the top-right corner and select "*Clear call history.*"

3.5 Voicemail and Call Forwarding

- **Setting Up Voicemail**: To set up voicemail, open the Phone app, tap the three-dot menu, and go to *Settings > Voicemail.* Follow the prompts to set up your voicemail box and greeting.

- **Accessing Voicemail**: To check your voicemail, press and hold the "1" key on the dial pad. Alternatively, you can access voicemail through the notifications panel if you have new messages.

- **Setting Up Call Forwarding**: In the Phone app, tap the three-dot menu and go to Settings > Call forwarding. Enter the number to which you want to forward your calls and configure the conditions (e.g., always forward, forward when busy).

- **Managing Voicemail Notifications**: In Settings > Voicemail, you can customize voicemail notification settings, including sound and vibration preferences.

Chapter 4: Text Messaging (SMS/MMS)

4.1 Sending and Receiving Text Messages

- **Opening the Messaging App**: Tap the messaging icon on your home screen or in the app drawer to open the Messages app.

- **Composing a New Message**:

  - Tap the "+" or "New Message" button usually located at the bottom or top of the screen.

  - In the recipient field, type the phone number or name of the contact you want to message. If the contact is saved in your phonebook, suggestions will appear as you type.

  - Tap the text field to start typing your message. Once done, tap the send icon (usually an arrow or paper plane) to send the message.

- **Receiving Messages**: When you receive a text message, a notification will appear at the top of your screen. Swipe down on the notification to view the message, or open the Messages app to read it.

- **Replying to Messages**: Open the conversation thread in the Messages app and type your reply in the text field at the bottom. Tap the send icon to send your reply.

4.2 Adding Attachments (Photos, Videos, etc.)

- **Composing an MMS**: To send an MMS, start by composing a new message or open an existing conversation.

  - Tap the attachment icon (usually a paperclip or camera icon) located near the text field.

  - Select the type of attachment you want to add: photo, video, audio, contact, or location.

- Choose the file from your gallery or capture a new photo/video using the camera.

- Once the attachment is added, type your message if desired, and tap the send icon to send the MMS.

4.3 Managing Conversations

- **Viewing Conversations**: Open the Messages app to see a list of your recent conversations. Tap a conversation to view the message history with that contact.

- **Deleting Messages**:

  - To delete a single message, tap and hold on the message within the conversation, then select "Delete."

  - To delete an entire conversation, go to the conversation list, tap and hold the conversation, then select "Delete."

- **Archiving Conversations**: To archive a conversation, tap and hold the conversation in the list, then select "Archive." Archived conversations are moved out of the main list but can be accessed later if needed.

- **Searching Messages**: Use the search bar at the top of the Messages app to find specific messages or conversations. Type keywords, contact names, or phone numbers to locate the desired message.

4.4 Customizing Message Settings

- **Notifications**:

  - Customize how you receive notifications for new messages by going to Settings > Notifications within the Messages app.

  - You can choose notification sounds, enable or disable vibration, and set preferences for pop-up notifications.

- **Message Organization**:
  - Enable or disable conversation categories to automatically organize messages into different categories like Personal, Business, OTPs, etc.
  - Use the "Starred Messages" feature to mark important messages for quick access later.
- **Advanced Messaging Settings**:
  - In the Messages app settings, you can enable or disable features like read receipts, delivery reports, and automatic retrieval of MMS.
  - Set up auto-reply messages for when you are busy or driving.
- **Blocking and Spam Protection**:
  - Block specific numbers from sending you messages by going to the conversation,

tapping the three-dot menu, and selecting "Block."

- Enable spam protection to filter out unwanted messages and identify potential spam.

4.5 Using RCS (Rich Communication Services)

- **What is RCS?**: RCS enhances traditional SMS/MMS messaging with features like read receipts, typing indicators, and high-resolution media sharing. Your carrier and the recipient's carrier must support RCS for these features to work.

- **Enabling RCS**: In the Messages app, go to Settings > Chat features. Follow the prompts to enable chat features, which include RCS.

- **Using RCS Features**:

- When RCS is enabled, you'll see features like read receipts and typing indicators in your conversations.

- You can send larger files, such as high-resolution photos and videos, without converting them to MMS.

4.6 Group Messaging

- **Creating a Group Chat**: Open the Messages app, tap the "+" or "New Message" button, and add multiple recipients in the "To" field. Type your message and tap the send icon to start the group chat.

- **Managing Group Chats**:

  - Add or remove participants by opening the group conversation, tapping the three-dot menu, and selecting "Group details."

  - Mute notifications for group chats by tapping the three-dot menu in the group conversation and selecting "Mute notifications."

- **Group Messaging Settings**: Customize group messaging settings by going to Settings > Advanced > Group messaging. Choose between sending group messages as individual SMS or as MMS (which allows all participants to see each other's responses).

Chapter 5: Managing Contacts

Efficiently managing your contacts is crucial for staying connected and organized. The Infinix Note 40 offers a variety of features to help you add, edit, organize, and synchronize your contacts. This chapter will provide a comprehensive guide on managing contacts on your device.

5.1 Adding and Editing Contacts

- **Adding a New Contact**:

  - Open the Contacts app from your home screen or app drawer.

  - Tap the "+" or "Add Contact" button usually located at the bottom or top of the screen.

  - Enter the contact's details, including name, phone number, email address, and any additional information like company, job title, and address.

- Tap "Save" to add the contact to your phonebook.

- **Editing an Existing Contact**:

  - Open the Contacts app and select the contact you wish to edit.

  - Tap the "Edit" button, usually represented by a pencil icon.

  - Update the necessary details and tap "Save" to apply the changes.

- **Adding a Photo to a Contact**:

  - While editing a contact, tap the photo icon to add or change the contact's picture.

  - Select a photo from your gallery or take a new one using the camera.

  - Adjust the photo as needed and tap "Save."

5.2 Creating Groups

- **Creating a Contact Group**:

    - Open the Contacts app and tap the menu icon (three horizontal lines or dots).

    - Select "Groups" and then tap "Create" or "Add Group."

    - Enter a name for the group and tap "Save."

    - Add contacts to the group by selecting them from your contact list and tapping "Done."

- **Managing Contact Groups**:

    - To edit a group, open the Groups section, select the group, and tap "Edit."

    - Add or remove contacts from the group as needed and tap "Save."

    - To delete a group, select the group, tap the menu icon, and choose "Delete."

5.3 Searching for Contacts

- **Using the Search Bar**:

    - Open the Contacts app and use the search bar at the top of the screen to find a contact.

    - Type the contact's name, phone number, or email address to filter your contacts.

    - Tap the desired contact from the search results to view their details.

- **Using Voice Search**:

    - Tap the microphone icon in the search bar and speak the contact's name or details.

    - Your device will search your contacts and display the matching results.

5.4 Syncing Contacts

- **Syncing with Google Account**:

    - Open the Settings app and go to "Accounts" or "Users & Accounts."

- Select your Google account and make sure "Sync Contacts" is enabled.

- Your contacts will automatically sync with your Google account, allowing you to access them across multiple devices.

- **Importing Contacts from SIM Card**:

  - Open the Contacts app and tap the menu icon.

  - Select "Import/Export" and then "Import from SIM card."

  - Choose the account where you want to save the imported contacts and select the contacts to import.

- **Exporting Contacts to SIM Card or Storage**:

  - Open the Contacts app and tap the menu icon.

- Select "Import/Export" and then "Export to SIM card" or "Export to storage."

- Choose the contacts to export and follow the prompts to complete the process.

• **Syncing with Other Accounts**:

- You can sync contacts from other accounts such as Microsoft Exchange, social media accounts, and more.

- Go to "Accounts" in the Settings app, select "Add account," and follow the instructions to set up the account.

- Ensure "Sync Contacts" is enabled for the added account.

5.5 Merging Duplicate Contacts

• **Automatic Merging**:

- Open the Contacts app and tap the menu icon.

- Select "Merge & fix" (if available) to let your device automatically find and merge duplicate contacts.

- **Manual Merging**:

  - Open the Contacts app and identify duplicate contacts.

  - Select one of the duplicates, tap "Edit," and then tap "Link contacts."

  - Select the duplicate contact to merge the details into a single entry.

- **Unlinking Contacts**:

  - If contacts were merged incorrectly, open the merged contact, tap "Edit," and then tap "Unlink contacts."

  - Select the contacts to unlink and save the changes.

5.6 Deleting Contacts

- **Deleting a Single Contact**:

  - Open the Contacts app and select the contact you wish to delete.

  - Tap the menu icon and choose "Delete."

  - Confirm the deletion to remove the contact from your phonebook.

- **Deleting Multiple Contacts**:

  - Open the Contacts app and tap the menu icon.

  - Select "Delete" or "Delete multiple" and choose the contacts to delete.

  - Tap "Delete" and confirm the action.

5.7 Contact Backup and Restore

- **Backing Up Contacts**:

- Use Google Drive or another cloud service to back up your contacts.

- Go to the Contacts app, tap the menu icon, and select "Settings."

- Tap "Export" and choose to export your contacts to a .vcf file.

- Save the .vcf file to your Google Drive or another cloud storage service.

- **Restoring Contacts**:

  - Open the Contacts app, tap the menu icon, and select "Settings."

  - Tap "Import" and choose to import contacts from a .vcf file.

  - Locate the backup file from your Google Drive or other storage and follow the prompts to restore your contacts.

Chapter 6: Capturing Photos and Videos

The Infinix Note 40 is equipped with advanced camera capabilities that allow you to take stunning photos and videos. This chapter will provide a detailed guide on how to make the most out of your device's camera, covering basic to advanced functionalities.

6.1 Taking Photos in Auto Mode

- **Launching the Camera App**:

  - Open the Camera app from your home screen or app drawer.

  - Alternatively, you can quickly access the camera by double-pressing the power button (if enabled in settings).

- **Auto Mode Overview**:

  - Auto Mode is the default setting that automatically adjusts the camera settings for optimal photos.

- The camera will automatically detect the scene and adjust the exposure, focus, and color balance.

- **Capturing Photos**:
    - Point your camera at the subject you wish to capture.
    - Tap on the screen to focus on a specific area, if necessary.
    - Press the shutter button to take the photo.
    - The photo will be saved to your gallery.

- **Using Flash**:
    - Tap the flash icon in the camera interface to toggle between Auto, On, and Off.
    - Use flash in low-light conditions to enhance the brightness of your photos.

6.2 Using Different Camera Modes

- **Portrait Mode**:

  - Select Portrait Mode from the camera modes menu.

  - This mode creates a depth-of-field effect, blurring the background to make the subject stand out.

  - Ensure the subject is within the recommended distance for optimal results.

  - Press the shutter button to take a portrait photo.

- **Macro Mode** (if applicable):

  - Select Macro Mode from the camera modes menu.

  - This mode allows you to capture close-up shots with great detail.

- Position the camera close to the subject and ensure it is in focus.
- Press the shutter button to capture the macro shot.

- **Night Mode**:
  - Select Night Mode from the camera modes menu.
  - This mode is designed for low-light conditions, reducing noise and enhancing details.
  - Hold the camera steady or use a tripod for the best results.
  - Press the shutter button to take the photo, allowing the camera a few seconds to capture more light.

- **Panorama Mode**:

- Select Panorama Mode from the camera modes menu.

- This mode captures wide-angle photos by stitching multiple images together.

- Press the shutter button and slowly move the camera in one direction.

- Follow the on-screen guide to keep the camera steady and level.

- The camera will automatically stop when the panorama is complete.

6.3 Recording Videos

- **Standard Video Recording**:

  - Open the Camera app and switch to Video mode.

  - Tap the red record button to start recording.

  - Press the red button again to stop recording.

- The video will be saved to your gallery.

- **Using Different Video Resolutions**:

  - Tap the settings icon in the camera interface and select Video Resolution.

  - Choose from available resolutions like 1440p, 1080p, or 720p.

  - Higher resolutions provide better quality but take up more storage space.

- **Using Flash During Video Recording**:

  - Tap the flash icon in the camera interface to enable or disable flash for video recording.

  - Use flash in low-light conditions to illuminate your subject.

6.4 Using Flash, Zoom, and HDR

- **Flash**:

- Use the flash settings for photos or videos in low-light conditions to brighten your subject.

- Toggle between Auto, On, and Off based on your needs.

- **Zoom**:

  - Pinch to zoom in and out on the camera interface.

  - Use the on-screen slider to adjust zoom levels smoothly.

  - Note that digital zoom can reduce image quality, so use sparingly for best results.

- **HDR (High Dynamic Range)**:

  - HDR mode captures multiple exposures and combines them for a balanced photo.

  - Tap the HDR icon in the camera interface to enable or disable HDR.

- Use HDR in high-contrast scenes, like landscapes with bright skies and dark shadows.

6.5 Advanced Camera Settings

- **Grid Lines**:
  - Enable grid lines from the camera settings to help compose your shots.
  - Grid lines help you apply the rule of thirds for balanced and aesthetically pleasing photos.

- **AI Scene Detection**:
  - The camera automatically detects the scene and adjusts settings for the best results.
  - Enable or disable AI Scene Detection from the camera settings.

- **Exposure Compensation**:

- Adjust exposure manually to control the brightness of your photos.

- Tap the screen to focus, then slide the exposure bar up or down to increase or decrease brightness.

6.6 Customizing Camera Settings

- **Photo and Video Resolution**:

  - Access camera settings and choose the desired photo and video resolution.

  - Higher resolutions offer better quality but require more storage.

- **Aspect Ratio**:

  - Select from different aspect ratios (e.g., 16:9, 4:3) based on your preference.

  - Change the aspect ratio in the camera settings.

- **White Balance and Exposure Controls**:

- Manually adjust white balance to match the lighting conditions.
- Use preset options like Auto, Daylight, Cloudy, Tungsten, and Fluorescent.

• **Image Quality**:

- Choose between standard and high image quality.
- Higher quality results in better photos but larger file sizes.

6.7 Reviewing and Editing Photos and Videos

• **Gallery App**:

- Open the Gallery app to view your captured photos and videos.
- Tap on any photo or video to view it in full screen.

• **Basic Editing**:

- Tap the edit icon to access basic editing tools.

- Crop, rotate, adjust brightness, contrast, saturation, and apply filters.

- **Advanced Editing**:

  - Use advanced editing apps available on the Play Store for more detailed adjustments.

  - Apps like Adobe Lightroom, Snapseed, and VSCO offer comprehensive editing features.

Chapter 7: Exploring Advanced Camera Features

The Infinix Note 40 is designed with advanced camera features that allow you to capture professional-quality photos and videos. In this chapter, we will delve into the advanced functionalities of your camera, including Pro Mode, Macro Lens, Slow-Motion Recording, and AI Photography.

7.1 Pro Mode for Manual Controls

- **Accessing Pro Mode**:

  - Open the Camera app and swipe through the available modes until you find Pro Mode.

  - Select Pro Mode to access manual controls for advanced photography.

- **Manual Settings**:

  - **ISO**: Adjust the camera's sensitivity to light. Lower ISO (e.g., 100) is ideal for bright conditions, while higher ISO (e.g., 800) is suitable for low-light environments.

- **Shutter Speed**: Control the amount of time the camera's shutter remains open. Fast shutter speeds (e.g., 1/1000s) freeze motion, while slow speeds (e.g., 1/30s) allow more light and create motion blur.

- **Aperture (f-stop)**: On phones, this setting is typically fixed. The Infinix Note 40's wide aperture allows for better low-light performance and depth-of-field effects.

- **White Balance**: Adjust to match the lighting conditions. Options include Auto, Daylight, Cloudy, Incandescent, and Fluorescent.

- **Focus**: Manually control the focus to ensure your subject is sharp. Use the focus slider to adjust as needed.

- **Taking Photos in Pro Mode**:

    - Set your desired manual settings based on the shooting environment.

    - Compose your shot and tap the screen to focus if necessary.

    - Press the shutter button to capture the photo.

7.2 Using the Macro Lens

- **Accessing Macro Mode**:

    - Open the Camera app and select Macro Mode from the available options.

    - This mode allows you to take close-up shots with enhanced detail.

- **Taking Macro Photos**:

    - Position the camera close to the subject, ideally within 3-5 cm.

- Ensure the subject is in focus. Use manual focus if needed.
- Press the shutter button to capture the photo.
- Macro Mode is perfect for capturing intricate details of small objects like flowers, insects, or textures.

7.3 Slow-Motion Recording

- **Accessing Slow-Motion Mode**:
  - Open the Camera app and swipe to find Slow-Motion Mode.
  - Select Slow-Motion to begin recording at a high frame rate.

- **Recording Slow-Motion Videos**:
  - Press the record button to start capturing slow-motion footage.

- Move the camera smoothly and avoid rapid movements to ensure clear and stable slow-motion video.

- Press the record button again to stop recording.

- Slow-Motion Mode is ideal for capturing fast-moving subjects like sports, pets, or water splashes.

7.4 AI Photography Made Easy: Enhance Your Photos with Intelligence

- **AI Scene Detection**:

  - The camera automatically detects the scene and adjusts settings for optimal results.

  - Common scenes include landscapes, portraits, food, and night shots.

  - Ensure AI Scene Detection is enabled in the camera settings.

- **AI Beautification**:

    - This feature enhances facial features and skin tones for more flattering portraits.

    - Open the Camera app and select Beauty Mode.

    - Adjust the beautification levels to your preference.

    - Press the shutter button to capture enhanced portraits.

- **AI HDR**:

    - High Dynamic Range (HDR) combines multiple exposures to create balanced photos with detail in both shadows and highlights.

    - Enable HDR in the camera settings or select Auto HDR.

- HDR is particularly useful in high-contrast scenes like sunsets or backlit subjects.

7.5 Advanced Camera Settings and Customization

- **Customizing Photo and Video Resolution**:

  - Access camera settings and select your preferred resolution.

  - Higher resolutions provide better quality but use more storage.

  - Choose from options like 1440p, 1080p, or 720p for videos.

- **Adjusting Image Quality**:

  - Select between standard and high image quality.

  - Higher quality settings result in better photos but larger file sizes.

- **White Balance and Exposure Controls**:

- Manually adjust white balance to match lighting conditions.
- Use preset options like Auto, Daylight, Cloudy, Tungsten, and Fluorescent.
- Adjust exposure compensation to control the brightness of your photos.

7.6 Reviewing and Editing Photos and Videos

- **Reviewing Captured Media**:
  - Open the Gallery app to view your photos and videos.
  - Tap on any media file to view it in full screen.

- **Basic Editing Tools**:
  - Tap the edit icon to access basic editing features.
  - Crop, rotate, adjust brightness, contrast, saturation, and apply filters.

- **Advanced Editing Apps**:

  - Use third-party apps for more advanced editing capabilities.

  - Popular apps include Adobe Lightroom, Snapseed, and VSCO.

  - These apps offer features like selective adjustments, advanced filters, and professional-grade editing tools.

Chapter 8: Camera Settings and Customization

The Infinix Note 40's camera offers a wide array of settings and customization options to help you tailor your photography experience. This chapter will guide you through the various settings and features available, ensuring you get the best possible results from your camera.

8.1 Adjusting Photo and Video Resolution

- **Accessing Resolution Settings**:

  - Open the Camera app.

  - Tap the settings icon (usually represented by a gear or three dots) to access camera settings.

  - Select "Resolution" or "Photo/Video Size" from the menu.

- **Photo Resolution**:

- Choose from various resolution options. Higher resolutions (e.g., 108 MP) provide more detail but result in larger file sizes.

- Use lower resolutions (e.g., 12 MP) for everyday photos to save storage space.

- Consider the balance between quality and storage based on your needs.

- **Video Resolution**:

  - Options typically include 1440p QHD, 1080p Full HD, and 720p HD.

  - Higher resolutions offer better video quality but consume more storage and battery.

  - Select 1440p for high-quality recordings, 1080p for a good balance of quality and file size, and 720p for extended recording sessions.

8.2 Customizing Image Quality

- **Standard vs. High Quality**:

  - Open the Camera app and access settings.

  - Find the "Image Quality" option and choose between Standard and High Quality.

  - High Quality enhances detail and color accuracy but increases file size.

- **Image Compression**:

  - Adjust the level of image compression in settings.

  - Lower compression results in higher quality images but larger file sizes.

  - Higher compression saves space but may reduce image quality.

8.3 White Balance and Exposure Controls

- **White Balance**:

- White balance ensures that colors appear natural under different lighting conditions.

- Access white balance settings through the Camera app.

- Choose from presets like Auto, Daylight, Cloudy, Incandescent, and Fluorescent.

- Auto mode works well in most situations, but manually select a preset to match specific lighting conditions.

- **Exposure Compensation**:

  - Exposure compensation adjusts the brightness of your photos.

  - In the Camera app, look for the exposure compensation slider, often represented by a +/- icon.

  - Increase exposure to brighten the image or decrease it to darken.

- Use exposure compensation to correct backlit scenes or when dealing with high-contrast lighting.

8.4 Using HDR (High Dynamic Range)

- **What is HDR?**:

  - HDR combines multiple exposures to produce a single image with balanced lighting.

  - It enhances details in both shadows and highlights.

- **Enabling HDR**:

  - Open the Camera app and find HDR settings.

  - Choose Auto HDR, On, or Off.

  - Auto HDR activates automatically in challenging lighting conditions, while On forces HDR for every shot.

- **Best Practices for HDR**:

    - Use HDR in high-contrast scenes like sunsets, landscapes, and backlit subjects.

    - Keep the camera steady to avoid ghosting effects.

    - Review HDR images for natural appearance; adjust settings if colors look too vibrant or unnatural.

8.5 Focus and Depth of Field

- **Autofocus**:

    - The Infinix Note 40's autofocus system automatically adjusts focus based on the scene.

    - Ensure autofocus is enabled in the Camera app settings.

    - Tap the screen to manually focus on a specific subject.

- **Manual Focus**:
  - In Pro Mode, use the focus slider to manually adjust focus.
  - Manual focus is useful for macro photography or when precise control is needed.
- **Depth of Field**:
  - Create a shallow depth of field by using a wide aperture (low f-stop) in Pro Mode.
  - This technique blurs the background, making the subject stand out.
  - Ideal for portraits and close-up shots.

8.6 Flash Settings
- **Flash Modes**:
  - Open the Camera app and access flash settings.

- Options typically include Auto, On, Off, and Torch (continuous light).

- **Using Flash Effectively**:

  - Use Auto mode to let the camera decide when flash is needed.

  - Turn flash On in low-light conditions or Off to avoid harsh lighting.

  - Torch mode is useful for video recording in dark environments.

- **Avoiding Flash Issues**:

  - Be cautious of red-eye effect when using flash for portraits.

  - Maintain a reasonable distance from the subject to avoid overexposure.

8.7 Image Stabilization

- **Electronic Image Stabilization (EIS)**:

- EIS helps reduce blur caused by camera shake.
- Enable EIS in the Camera app settings if available.

- **Using Tripods and Gimbals**:
    - For maximum stability, use a tripod or gimbal.
    - These tools are essential for long-exposure shots and smooth video recording.

8.8 Customizing Camera Shortcuts

- **Quick Access**:
    - Customize camera shortcuts for quick access to your favorite modes and settings.
    - Open the Camera app, go to settings, and find "Customize Shortcuts."

- **Adding and Removing Shortcuts**:

- Add frequently used features like Pro Mode, HDR, or Flash to the main interface.

- Remove shortcuts you rarely use to streamline the camera interface.

8.9 Reviewing and Managing Captured Media

- **Viewing Photos and Videos**:

  - Open the Gallery app to review captured media.

  - Tap on a photo or video to view it in full screen.

- **Organizing Media**:

  - Create albums to organize photos and videos.

  - Use the Gallery app's sorting options to arrange media by date, location, or tags.

- **Editing Tools**:

- Use built-in editing tools to enhance your photos and videos.
- Basic edits include cropping, rotating, adjusting brightness, contrast, and applying filters.

- **Advanced Editing Apps**:
  - For more advanced editing, consider third-party apps like Adobe Lightroom, Snapseed, and VSCO.
  - These apps offer features like selective adjustments, advanced filters, and professional-grade tools.

8.10 Backing Up Photos and Videos

- **Cloud Storage**:
  - Use cloud services like Google Photos, OneDrive, or Dropbox to back up your media.

- Enable automatic backup in the app settings to ensure your photos and videos are always safe.

- **Local Backup**:

    - Transfer photos and videos to a computer or external storage device regularly.

    - Use USB or wireless transfer methods to back up media.

Maximizing Functionality

Chapter 9: Fingerprint Unlock and Facial Recognition

The Infinix Note 40 offers advanced biometric security features to enhance your device's security while providing quick and convenient access. In this chapter, we will delve into the setup, usage, and optimization of both the fingerprint unlock and facial recognition features.

9.1 Setting Up Fingerprint Unlock

Initial Setup:

- **Step 1:** Open the **Settings** app on your Infinix Note 40.

- **Step 2:** Navigate to **Security & Privacy**.

- **Step 3:** Select **Fingerprint Unlock**.

- **Step 4:** You may be prompted to set a backup PIN, pattern, or password if you haven't already.

- **Step 5:** Follow the on-screen instructions to register your fingerprint. Place your finger on the in-display fingerprint sensor and lift it repeatedly until the registration is complete.

- **Step 6:** After successful registration, you can add more fingerprints by selecting **Add Fingerprint**.

Optimizing Fingerprint Recognition:

- **Clean the Sensor:** Ensure the in-display fingerprint sensor is clean and free of smudges or dirt.

- **Use Multiple Angles:** Register the same fingerprint multiple times from different angles to improve recognition accuracy.

- **Dry Hands:** Ensure your hands are dry when using the fingerprint sensor, as moisture can affect its performance.

Using Fingerprint Unlock:

- **Unlocking the Phone:** Simply place your registered finger on the in-display fingerprint sensor. The phone should unlock almost instantly.

- **App Authentication:** Use your fingerprint to authenticate in supported apps, enhancing security without compromising convenience.

- **Quick Actions:** Some apps and settings allow you to use the fingerprint sensor for quick actions, such as taking photos or accessing secure folders.

9.2 Setting Up Facial Recognition

Initial Setup:

- **Step 1:** Open the **Settings** app.

- **Step 2:** Navigate to **Security & Privacy**.

- **Step 3:** Select **Face Unlock**.

- **Step 4:** Set a backup PIN, pattern, or password if prompted.

- **Step 5:** Follow the on-screen instructions to register your face. Hold the phone at eye level and ensure your face is well-lit and within the frame until the registration is complete.

Optimizing Facial Recognition:

- **Good Lighting:** Ensure you set up facial recognition in a well-lit environment for better accuracy.

- **Clear View:** Remove any obstructions like glasses or hats during the setup process.

- **Update Regularly:** Re-register your face periodically, especially if your appearance changes significantly (e.g., growing a beard or getting a new hairstyle).

Using Facial Recognition:

- **Unlocking the Phone:** Raise your phone to eye level. The front camera will recognize your face and unlock the device.

- **App Authentication:** Use facial recognition to authenticate in supported apps, providing a seamless and secure login experience.

- **Attention Awareness:** Enable the **Require Eyes to be Open** setting to enhance security, ensuring that the phone only unlocks when your eyes are open and looking at the screen.

9.3 Enhancing Security with Biometric Data

Combining Biometric Methods:

- **Multi-Layer Security:** For enhanced security, combine both fingerprint unlock and facial recognition. This provides multiple layers of biometric authentication.

- **Smart Lock:** Use Android's Smart Lock feature to keep your device unlocked in trusted environments, such as at home or when connected to a trusted Bluetooth device.

Protecting Your Biometric Data:

- **Secure Storage:** Infinix Note 40 securely stores biometric data in a dedicated secure enclave within the device, ensuring it cannot be accessed by unauthorized apps or external threats.

- **Regular Updates:** Keep your device's software up to date to ensure you have the latest security patches and improvements.

9.4 Troubleshooting Biometric Issues

Fingerprint Sensor Issues:

- **Recalibrate Fingerprints:** If your fingerprints are not being recognized, try deleting and re-registering them.

- **Sensor Cleanliness:** Regularly clean the fingerprint sensor to ensure it works accurately.

- **Environmental Factors:** Dry or moisturize your hands if the sensor struggles to read your fingerprint.

Facial Recognition Issues:

- **Re-register Face:** If facial recognition fails frequently, re-register your face in various lighting conditions.

- **Camera Cleanliness:** Ensure the front camera is clean and unobstructed.

- **Check Lighting:** Use facial recognition in well-lit environments to improve accuracy.

General Tips:

- **Restart Device:** Restart your device if biometric features are not working correctly.

- **Check Updates:** Ensure your device's software is up to date, as updates may fix issues with biometric recognition.

9.5 Advanced Security Settings

Secure Folder:

- **Setup:** Create a secure folder in the settings to store sensitive files and apps. Protect it with fingerprint or facial recognition for additional security.

- **Access:** Access the secure folder via the app drawer or settings, requiring biometric authentication each time.

App Lock:

- **Setup:** Enable app lock in the security settings to protect individual apps with your fingerprint or face.

- **Usage:** Each time you open a protected app, you will be prompted to authenticate using your chosen biometric method.

Chapter 10: Connecting to Wi-Fi and Sharing Your Connection

In today's connected world, having seamless access to the internet is crucial. The Infinix Note 40 offers robust Wi-Fi capabilities, enabling you to connect to wireless networks easily and even share your internet connection with other devices. This chapter will guide you through setting up Wi-Fi, optimizing your connection, and sharing it securely.

10.1 Connecting to Wi-Fi Networks

Step-by-Step Guide to Connect:

1. **Open Settings:**

   - Go to the **Settings** on your phone

2. **Select Wi-Fi:**

   - Tap on **Network & Internet**, then select **Wi-Fi** or **Tap on Internet**

- **Alternatively**, *swipe down from top screen to see the list **then** tap internet to see Wi-Fi then toggle to put it on*

3. **Enable Wi-Fi:**

    - Toggle the Wi-Fi switch to turn it on. Your phone will automatically start scanning for available networks.

4. **Choose a Network:**

    - From the list of available networks, select the Wi-Fi network you wish to connect to.

5. **Enter Password:**

87

- If the network is secured, you will be prompted to enter a password. Type in the correct password and tap **Connect**.

6. **Connection Status:**

    - Once connected, you will see the Wi-Fi icon in the status bar, indicating a successful connection.

Optimizing Wi-Fi Performance:

- **Strong Signal:** Choose a network with a strong signal to ensure a stable connection. The signal strength is indicated by the number of bars next to the network name.

- **Network Preference:** In the Wi-Fi settings, enable **Network Preferences** to automatically connect to high-quality public networks.

- **Frequency Bands:** If available, use the 5GHz frequency band for faster speeds and less interference compared to the 2.4GHz band.

10.2 Sharing Your Wi-Fi Connection

The Infinix Note 40 can act as a Wi-Fi hotspot, allowing you to share your mobile data connection with other devices. Here's how to set up and manage your hotspot.

Setting Up a Mobile Hotspot:

1. **Open Settings:**

    - Go to the **Settings** icon.

2. **Select Hotspot & Tethering:**

    - Navigate to **Network & Internet**, then tap **Hotspot & Tethering**.

3. **Enable Hotspot:**

    - Toggle the switch next to **Wi-Fi Hotspot** to turn it on.

4. **Configure Hotspot Settings:**

    - Tap on **Wi-Fi Hotspot** to access and configure settings.

    - **Network Name (SSID):** Enter a name for your hotspot.

    - **Security:** Select a security type (WPA2 is recommended for better security).

    - **Password:** Set a strong password to prevent unauthorized access.

5. **Connect Devices:**

- Other devices can now connect to your hotspot by selecting your network name and entering the password you set.

Managing Connected Devices:

- **View Connected Devices:** In the hotspot settings, you can see a list of devices currently connected to your hotspot.

- **Block Devices:** If you notice any unauthorized device, you can block it directly from the list of connected devices.

- **Data Usage:** Monitor data usage to ensure you don't exceed your data plan limit. This can be managed within the **Hotspot & Tethering** settings.

10.3 Advanced Wi-Fi Settings

Wi-Fi Preferences:

- **Auto-Connect:** Set your phone to automatically connect to high-quality public Wi-Fi networks.

- **Network Notifications:** Enable notifications to alert you when a strong public Wi-Fi network is available.

Wi-Fi Direct:

- **Setup Wi-Fi Direct:** Wi-Fi Direct allows for direct data transfer between devices without needing a wireless access point. This can be accessed in the Wi-Fi settings under **Wi-Fi Direct**.

- **Connecting Devices:** Select the device you want to connect to and follow the prompts to establish a connection.

Advanced Settings:

- **IP Settings:** In the Wi-Fi network's advanced settings, you can manually configure the IP address and DNS settings if needed.

- **Proxy Settings:** Configure a proxy for specific Wi-Fi networks to manage internet traffic.

10.4 Troubleshooting Wi-Fi Issues

Common Issues and Solutions:

- **Unable to Connect to Wi-Fi:**

  - **Check Password:** Ensure you are entering the correct password.

  - **Restart Router:** Restart your Wi-Fi router to refresh the connection.

  - **Forget Network:** Go to the Wi-Fi settings, tap on the network name, and select **Forget Network**. Then, reconnect by entering the password again.

- **Slow Connection:**

- **Proximity:** Move closer to the Wi-Fi router to improve signal strength.

- **Interference:** Reduce interference by moving away from other electronic devices that might affect Wi-Fi signals.

- **Network Traffic:** Check if multiple devices are using the network, which could slow down the connection. Limit the number of connected devices if necessary.

• **Wi-Fi Keeps Dropping:**

- **Update Firmware:** Ensure your router's firmware is up to date.

- **Power Cycle Devices:** Restart both your phone and the router.

- **Network Settings Reset:** As a last resort, reset network settings on your phone. Go to

Settings > System > Reset Options > Reset Wi-Fi, mobile & Bluetooth.

Advanced Troubleshooting:

- **Wi-Fi Analyzer Apps:** Use apps like Wi-Fi Analyzer to identify the best channels for your Wi-Fi network and reduce interference.

- **Check Router Settings:** Access your router's settings to ensure optimal configurations, such as channel selection and bandwidth allocation.

Chapter 11: Pairing with Bluetooth Devices

Bluetooth technology enables you to wirelessly connect your Infinix Note 40 to various devices, including headphones, speakers, cars, and even other phones. This chapter will guide you through the process of pairing, connecting, and managing Bluetooth devices, as well as transferring files via Bluetooth.

11.1 Connecting to Bluetooth Headphones or Speakers

Step-by-Step Guide to Pairing:

1. **Turn on Bluetooth:**

   - Open the **Settings** app on your phone

   - Tap on **Connected devices**, then select **Bluetooth** and toggle the switch to turn it on.

2. **Make Device Discoverable:**

- On the device you want to pair (e.g., headphones or speaker), ensure it is in pairing mode. This usually involves holding down a specific button until a light starts blinking or an audible tone is heard. Refer to the device's manual for exact instructions.

3. **Scan for Devices:**

    - On your Infinix Note 40, tap **Pair new device**. Your phone will start scanning for nearby Bluetooth devices.

4. **Select the Device:**

    - From the list of available devices, tap on the name of the device you want to pair with.

5. **Confirm Pairing:**

    - A pairing request will appear on your phone. Tap **Pair** to confirm. You may be asked to enter a PIN or confirm a code, especially with more secure devices.

6. **Connection Confirmation:**

- Once paired, you'll see the device listed under **Paired devices** in the Bluetooth settings. A notification may also appear confirming the connection.

Using Bluetooth Audio Devices:

- **Audio Output:** Once connected, your phone's audio will automatically route to the Bluetooth device. You can control volume and playback directly from the connected device or your phone.

- **Media Controls:** Use media control buttons on your Bluetooth headphones or speakers to play, pause, skip tracks, and adjust volume without touching your phone.

11.2 Transferring Files via Bluetooth

Step-by-Step Guide to File Transfer:

1. **Enable Bluetooth:**

   - Ensure Bluetooth is turned on both on your phone and the device you want to transfer files to.

2. **Pair Devices:**

   - Pair the devices if they are not already paired. Follow the pairing process detailed in section 11.1.

3. **Select Files:**

   - Open the file manager or gallery app on your Infinix Note 40.

   - Select the file(s) you wish to send. You can usually select multiple files by long-pressing on one file and then tapping others.

4. **Send Files:**

- Tap the **Share** icon and select **Bluetooth** from the sharing options.
- Choose the device from the list of available paired devices.

5. **Accept Transfer:**

    - On the receiving device, accept the file transfer request. Depending on the device, this may involve tapping **Accept** or a similar option.

6. **Transfer Completion:**

    - Wait for the transfer to complete. A notification will appear once the file transfer is successful.

Managing Received Files:

- **Location:** Received files are usually saved in the **Bluetooth** folder in the device's internal storage.

- **Access:** Use the file manager app to access and organize received files.

11.3 Managing Bluetooth Connections

Viewing Paired Devices:

- **Access List:** In the Bluetooth settings on your phone, you can view a list of all devices currently paired with your phone.

- **Device Information:** Tap on any paired device to see detailed information and options.

Unpairing Devices:

- **Unpairing:** To unpair a device, tap on the device name in the Bluetooth settings and select **Unpair**. This will remove the device from the list of paired devices.

Renaming Paired Devices:

- **Custom Name:** You can rename paired devices for easier identification. In the

Bluetooth settings, tap on the device name, then tap **Rename**. Enter the new name and confirm.

Advanced Bluetooth Settings:

- **Device Profiles:** Certain Bluetooth devices support multiple profiles (e.g., audio, calls, input devices). You can enable or disable specific profiles for each device in the advanced Bluetooth settings.

- **Dual Audio:** Some versions of Android and certain devices support dual audio, allowing you to connect and play audio on two Bluetooth devices simultaneously.

11.4 Troubleshooting Bluetooth Issues

Common Issues and Solutions:

- **Cannot Find Device:**

- **Check Distance:** Ensure the devices are within a reasonable range (usually up to 10 meters).

- **Discoverable Mode:** Make sure the device you want to pair is in discoverable mode.

- **Restart Devices:** Restart both your Infinix Note 40 and the device you are trying to connect to.

- **Connection Drops:**

  - **Interference:** Move away from other wireless devices that might be causing interference.

  - **Battery Level:** Ensure both devices have sufficient battery levels.

- **Poor Audio Quality:**

  - **Signal Strength:** Maintain a clear line of sight between the devices.

- **Audio Codec:** Use high-quality audio codecs like aptX if supported by both devices.

Advanced Troubleshooting:

- **Reset Network Settings:** If persistent issues occur, you might need to reset your phone's network settings. Go to **Settings** > **System** > **Reset Options** > **Reset Wi-Fi, mobile & Bluetooth**.

- **Software Updates:** Ensure both your phone and the Bluetooth device are running the latest software updates. Manufacturers often release updates to fix bugs and improve compatibility.

Chapter 12: Optimizing Battery Life

Your Infinix Note 40 comes equipped with a powerful 5000mAh battery, designed to keep you going throughout the day. However, to get the most out of your battery and extend its lifespan, it's essential to understand how to manage and optimize battery usage. This chapter covers detailed steps to monitor, save, and efficiently use your battery power.

12.1 Understanding Battery Usage

Battery Usage Screen:

- **Accessing Battery Usage:** Go to **Settings** > **Battery** > **Battery Usage**. This screen provides an overview of how your battery is being used by various apps and system processes.

- **Graph:** The battery usage graph shows the rate at which your battery is depleting. Spikes or rapid declines can indicate high power consumption.

- **App Usage:** Below the graph, you'll see a list of apps and their respective battery consumption percentages. Apps consuming unusually high amounts of battery should be checked for potential issues.

Identifying Battery Drainers:

- **High Consumption Apps:** Apps listed at the top of the battery usage list are the most power-hungry. Consider limiting their use or adjusting their settings.

- **Background Activity:** Apps running in the background can significantly impact battery life. Disable background activity for non-essential apps by going to **Settings** > **Apps** > **[App Name]** > **Battery** > **Background Restriction**.

12.2 Enabling Battery-Saving Features

Battery Saver Mode:

- **Activating Battery Saver:** Go to **Settings** > **Battery** > **Battery Saver**. Toggle the switch to turn it on. Battery Saver reduces background activity, limits certain features, and dims the display to extend battery life.

- **Automatic Activation:** You can set Battery Saver to turn on automatically at a specific battery percentage. Select **Set a schedule** and choose a threshold (e.g., 15%).

Adaptive Battery:

- **What It Does:** Adaptive Battery uses AI to learn your usage patterns and restricts battery usage for apps you don't use often. This helps extend battery life over time.

- **Enabling Adaptive Battery:** Go to **Settings** > **Battery** > **Adaptive Battery** and toggle the switch to turn it on.

Optimizing Individual App Settings:

- **App-Specific Battery Settings:** For apps that consume a lot of power, go to **Settings** > **Apps** > **[App Name]** > **Battery**. Here, you can restrict background activity or allow the app to use battery power freely.

- **Optimize Apps:** Go to **Settings** > **Battery** > **Battery Usage** > **More** > **Optimize Battery Usage**. This feature allows you to optimize battery use for all apps or specific apps.

12.3 Charging Your Phone

Charging Basics:

- **Use the Included Charger:** Always use the original charger and cable provided with your Infinix Note 40 to ensure safe and efficient charging.

- **Fast Charging:** The Infinix Note 40 supports 45W All-Round FastCharge2.0. To enable fast charging, ensure you are using a compatible charger. Go to **Settings** > **Battery** > **Fast Charging** and toggle the switch.

Wireless Charging:

- **Setup:** Place your phone on a compatible wireless charger. The Infinix Note 40 supports 20W wireless charging, which is efficient but slightly slower than wired fast charging.

- **Positioning:** Ensure the phone is properly aligned with the charging pad. Misalignment can result in slower charging or no charging at all.

Reverse Charging:

- **Using Your Phone as a Charger:** The Infinix Note 40 can wirelessly charge other devices. Go to **Settings** > **Battery** > **Reverse Charging** and toggle the switch. Place the other device on the back of your Infinix Note 40 to start charging.

- **Cables:** For wired reverse charging, use a USB-C to USB-C or USB-C to micro USB cable to connect the two devices.

Battery Health Tips:

- **Avoid Extreme Temperatures:** Keep your phone in environments with moderate temperatures. Extreme heat or cold can damage the battery.

- **Partial Charging:** Avoid fully discharging your battery regularly. Partial charging, between 20% and 80%, is ideal for battery longevity.

- **Remove Case While Charging:** If your phone tends to heat up while charging, consider removing the case to allow better heat dissipation.

Monitoring and Notifications:

- **Battery Health Notification:** The system will notify you if it detects any issues with your battery or charging process.

- **Battery Usage Notification:** If an app is consuming an unusually high amount of battery, you will receive a notification suggesting you take action.

XOS CUSTOMIZATION

Chapter 13: Personalizing Your XOS Experience

XOS, the custom skin from Infinix, provides a rich layer of customization over the standard Android experience, allowing you to personalize your Infinix Note 40 to fit your preferences and needs. This chapter covers detailed steps on how to modify themes, wallpapers, ringtones, and launcher settings to make your device truly yours.

13.1 Changing Themes and Wallpapers

Themes:

- **Accessing Themes**: Open the **XTheme** app from your app drawer. This app houses a variety of themes designed to alter the look and feel of your device comprehensively, including icons, fonts, and colors.

- **Browsing Themes**: Inside the XTheme app, browse through the available themes. Themes are often categorized by style, such as modern, classic, abstract, etc.

- **Downloading Themes:** Tap on a theme to view its details. If you like it, press **Download**. Some themes might be free, while others could require payment.

- **Applying Themes:** After downloading, select **Apply**. Your phone will immediately adopt the new visual style.

Wallpapers:

- **Changing Wallpapers from Settings:** Go to **Settings** > **Display** > **Wallpaper**. Here, you can choose from pre-installed wallpapers or use your own photos.

- **Dynamic and Live Wallpapers:** For a more dynamic look, select **Live Wallpapers** for animated backgrounds. Be mindful that live wallpapers might consume more battery.

- **Setting Custom Wallpapers:** To use a custom image, tap **Choose from Gallery** and select the desired image. Adjust the positioning and press **Set Wallpaper**. You can choose to apply it to the home screen, lock screen, or both.

13.2 Customizing Ringtones and Notifications

Ringtones:

- **Accessing Sound Settings:** Go to **Settings** > **Sound & Vibration** > **Ringtone**.

- **Choosing a Ringtone:** Browse through the list of pre-installed ringtones. Tap on a ringtone to preview it, then select **Apply** if you like it.

- **Custom Ringtones:** To use a custom ringtone, tap **Add from Files** and select a music file from your device. This allows for a truly personalized sound.

Notification Sounds:

- **Changing Notification Sounds:** Navigate to **Settings** > **Sound & Vibration** > **Notification Sound**. Here, you can select from various sounds provided by Infinix.

- **Custom Notification Sounds:** Similar to ringtones, you can add your own notification sounds by selecting **Add from Files**.

Alarm Tones:

- **Setting Alarm Tones:** Open the Clock app, set an alarm, and then tap **Alarm Sound**. You can choose from pre-installed tones or add custom sounds.

13.3 Adjusting Launcher Settings

Home Screen Layout:

- **Accessing Launcher Settings:** Long-press on an empty space on the home screen, then select **Settings** or open **Settings** > **Display** > **Home Screen**.

- **Grid Size:** Change the home screen grid size to adjust how many icons can fit on a single screen. Options typically include 4x5, 5x5, etc.

- **Icon Size:** Adjust the size of app icons to make them larger or smaller according to your preference.

App Drawer Customization:

- **Organizing Apps:** You can categorize apps into folders. Drag and drop apps on top of each other to create a folder, then name it appropriately.

- **Hiding Apps:** To hide certain apps from the app drawer, go to **Settings** > **Display** > **Home Screen** > **Hide Apps**. Select the apps you wish to hide.

Home Screen Transition Effects:

- **Changing Transition Effects:** Long-press on an empty space on the home screen, select **Effects**, and choose from a variety of transition effects such as slide, fade, cube, etc. These effects change how screens transition as you swipe left or right.

Custom Widgets:

- **Adding Widgets:** Long-press on an empty area on the home screen, then select **Widgets**. Browse through available widgets and add them to your home screen for quick access to information and apps.

- **Adjusting Widget Size:** Once a widget is placed, long-press it to resize it according to your preference.

Dock Customization:

- **Dock Settings:** Go to **Settings** > **Display** > **Home Screen** > **Dock**. You can adjust the number of icons in the dock and choose whether to display labels for dock icons.

Additional Customization Tips

Edge Lighting:

- **Enabling Edge Lighting:** Go to **Settings** > **Display** > **Edge Lighting**. This feature uses the screen edges to show notifications, providing a subtle yet elegant alert system.

- **Customizing Edge Lighting:** Choose different colors and patterns for edge lighting to personalize how notifications appear.

Navigation Gestures:

- **Switching Navigation Modes:** Go to **Settings** > **System** > **Gestures** > **System Navigation**. You can switch between navigation buttons and gesture-based navigation.

- **Gesture Customization:** Customize gestures for actions such as swiping up from the bottom for home, swiping from the sides for back, etc.

Chapter 14: Exploring Unique XOS Features

The Infinix Note 40's XOS is packed with unique features that enhance the functionality and user experience of your smartphone. This chapter provides a comprehensive guide to exploring and utilizing these features, ensuring you get the most out of your device.

14.1 Using the Folax Voice Assistant

Folax is Infinix's intelligent voice assistant designed to help you navigate your phone hands-free and perform various tasks using voice commands.

Setting Up Folax:

- **Activation:** Open the Folax app from your app drawer or activate it by saying "Hey Folax" (if voice activation is enabled).

- **Voice Training:** Follow the on-screen instructions to train Folax to recognize your voice. This step improves accuracy and ensures that Folax responds correctly to your commands.

- **Permissions:** Grant necessary permissions for Folax to access your contacts, messages, and other apps to provide a seamless experience.

Using Folax:

- **Making Calls and Sending Messages:** Say, "Hey Folax, call [contact name]" or "Hey Folax, send a message to [contact name]." Folax will initiate the call or open the messaging app for you.

- **Setting Reminders and Alarms:** Command Folax to set reminders or alarms, such as "Hey Folax, set a reminder for my meeting at 10 AM" or "Hey Folax, set an alarm for 6 AM."

- **Opening Apps:** Quickly access apps by saying, "Hey Folax, open [app name]."

- **Weather Updates and Information:** Ask for weather updates or general information, like "Hey Folax, what's the weather today?" or "Hey Folax, who won the football game?"

Customizing Folax:

- **Settings:** Access Folax settings through the app to customize voice activation phrases, language preferences, and other settings to suit your needs.

14.2 Enabling Lightning Multi-Window

Lightning Multi-Window allows you to multitask efficiently by running two apps simultaneously on the screen.

Activating Multi-Window:

- **Method 1: Recent Apps:** Open the Recent Apps menu by swiping up from the bottom of the screen or tapping the Recent Apps button.

Tap the app icon at the top of one of the apps, then select **Split Screen**.

- **Method 2: Edge Panel:** Swipe from the edge of the screen to access the Edge Panel (if enabled), then drag and drop apps into the split-screen view.

Using Multi-Window:

- **Adjusting Window Size:** Drag the divider between the two apps to resize each window to your preference.

- **Switching Apps:** Tap the app switcher icon to replace one of the apps in split-screen mode with another app from the Recent Apps menu or app drawer.

- **Exiting Multi-Window:** Drag the divider to the top or bottom of the screen to exit split-screen mode and return to full-screen mode.

Customizing Multi-Window:

- **Edge Panel Settings:** Go to **Settings** > **Display** > **Edge Panels** to customize the apps and tools available in the Edge Panel for quick access to Multi-Window mode.

14.3 Creating Custom Gestures

XOS allows you to create custom gestures to perform various actions quickly, providing a more intuitive and efficient way to use your phone.

Setting Up Custom Gestures:

- **Accessing Gestures:** Go to **Settings** > **System** > **Gestures**.

- **Available Gestures:** Explore available gestures such as double-tap to wake, swipe up for home, and others. Enable or disable each gesture based on your preferences.

Creating Custom Gestures:

- **Drawing Gestures:** In the Gestures menu, select **Custom Gestures**. Tap **Add Gesture**, then draw the gesture you want to use, such as a letter or shape.

- **Assigning Actions:** After creating a gesture, assign it an action, such as opening an app, calling a contact, or taking a screenshot. For example, you could draw an "M" to open the messaging app.

Using Custom Gestures:

- **Executing Gestures:** Once created, you can perform the custom gesture on the home screen or lock screen to trigger the assigned action. Ensure the screen is responsive and recognizes your gesture accurately.

- **Editing Gestures:** To modify or delete a custom gesture, return to **Settings** > **System** >

Gestures > **Custom Gestures**, select the gesture, and choose to edit or remove it.

Gesture Navigation:

- **Switching to Gesture Navigation:** Go to **Settings** > **System** > **Gestures** > **System Navigation**. Choose **Gesture Navigation** to replace the traditional navigation buttons with gestures.

- **Navigating with Gestures:** Learn the gestures for navigation, such as swiping up from the bottom for home, swiping from the sides for back, and swiping up and holding for the recent apps menu. This provides a more immersive and streamlined experience.

Enhancing Accessibility with Gestures:

- **Accessibility Features:** Explore additional accessibility gestures in **Settings** > **Accessibility**. Enable features like assistive touch, magnification gestures, and more to enhance usability for different needs.

Glossary of Phone Lingo

Accelerometer: A sensor in your phone that detects movement and orientation. It's used for various functions like adjusting screen orientation and motion-based controls.

AMOLED (Active Matrix Organic Light Emitting Diode): A type of display technology known for its vibrant colors, deep blacks, and energy efficiency, commonly used in high-end smartphones.

Android: A mobile operating system developed by Google, used by many smartphones and tablets, including the Infinix Note 40.

App Drawer: The section of the user interface where all installed applications are listed. It's usually accessed by swiping up on the home screen.

Aspect Ratio: The proportional relationship between a display's width and height. For example, a 20:9 aspect ratio means the display is 20 units wide for every 9 units tall.

Auto Mode: A camera mode where settings like exposure, focus, and white balance are automatically adjusted by the camera software.

Battery-Saving Features: Functions and settings designed to extend battery life by reducing power consumption, such as lowering screen brightness or disabling background processes.

Bluetooth: A wireless technology standard for exchanging data over short distances between devices, such as smartphones and headphones.

Corning Gorilla Glass: A brand of toughened glass designed to be scratch and impact resistant, commonly used as a protective layer for smartphone screens.

CPU (Central Processing Unit): The primary component of a computer or smartphone that performs most of the processing inside a device. The CPU of the Infinix Note 40 is an Octa-Core processor.

Dedicated Memory Card Slot: A separate slot for a microSD card, allowing users to expand the device's storage without sacrificing a SIM slot.

Edge Panel: A feature providing quick access to apps, tools, and other functions by swiping from the edge of the screen.

Fingerprint Sensor: A biometric security feature that uses your fingerprint to unlock the device and authenticate various functions.

Flash (Quad LED): An arrangement of four LEDs used to provide additional light for taking photos in low-light conditions.

Folax Voice Assistant: Infinix's intelligent voice assistant that helps you perform tasks using voice commands.

Gesture Navigation: A navigation method using swipe gestures instead of physical or on-screen buttons to interact with the phone's interface.

HDR (High Dynamic Range): A photography technique that enhances the contrast and color range of an image, making it more vibrant and detailed.

IR Blaster: An infrared transmitter that allows the smartphone to control devices like TVs and air conditioners by emulating a remote control.

Macro Lens: A camera lens designed for taking close-up shots with a high level of detail, typically used for photographing small subjects.

Mali-G57 MC2: The GPU (Graphics Processing Unit) used in the Infinix Note 40, responsible for rendering images and video.

Multi-Window: A feature that allows you to run and view two apps simultaneously on the screen, facilitating multitasking.

NFC (Near Field Communication): A wireless technology enabling short-range communication between devices for functions like contactless payments and data transfer.

Octa-Core Processor: A CPU with eight cores, allowing for better multitasking and performance.

Panorama: A camera mode that captures wide-angle photos by stitching together multiple images taken while panning the camera.

Peak Brightness: The maximum brightness level a display can achieve, useful for readability in bright conditions.

PWM Dimming (Pulse Width Modulation): A technique used to control the brightness of the display by varying the width of the light pulses.

QHD (Quad High Definition): A resolution of 1440p, offering four times the detail of standard HD (720p) resolution.

RAM (Random Access Memory): A type of memory used to store data that is being actively used or processed by the CPU. The Infinix Note 40 has 8 GB of RAM, with an additional 8 GB of virtual RAM.

Reverse Charging: A feature that allows your phone to charge other devices, acting as a power bank.

SIM Card: A small card inserted into a phone to provide cellular network connectivity.

Slow-Motion Recording: A camera feature that records video at a higher frame rate, allowing the playback to be slowed down for dramatic effect.

Splash Resistant: A feature indicating that the device can withstand minor exposure to water, such as light rain or splashes.

Touch Sampling Rate: The frequency at which the screen registers touch inputs, with a higher rate providing faster and more responsive touch performance.

USB-C: A type of USB connector that is reversible and supports faster data transfer and charging speeds.

UFS (Universal Flash Storage): A type of storage technology that offers faster read and write speeds compared to older storage types like eMMC. The Infinix Note 40 uses UFS 2.2.

VoLTE (Voice over LTE): A technology allowing voice calls to be made over the 4G LTE network, resulting in higher-quality calls and faster connection times.

White Balance: A camera setting that adjusts the colors to appear more natural based on the lighting conditions.

XOS: The custom user interface developed by Infinix, based on the Android operating system, offering additional features and customization options.

Zoom: A camera function that allows you to get closer to the subject without physically moving, available in digital or optical forms depending on the camera.

CONCLUSION

The Infinix Note 40 represents a remarkable blend of innovation, performance, and style. Throughout this comprehensive guide, we've explored the many facets that make this device a standout choice in the crowded smartphone market. From unboxing your new phone and setting it up to mastering its advanced camera features and personalizing your XOS experience, the Infinix Note 40 is designed to cater to both tech enthusiasts and everyday users alike.

One of the key highlights of the Infinix Note 40 is its impressive AMOLED display, offering vibrant colors and sharp visuals that bring your content to life. The high refresh rate ensures smooth scrolling and an immersive viewing experience, whether you're gaming, streaming videos, or simply browsing the web.

The camera system is another standout feature, with its 108 MP main sensor capturing stunning photos and videos. The advanced modes and AI enhancements allow you to unleash your creativity and capture moments in unprecedented detail. Whether you're a photography enthusiast or just someone who loves to share memories, the Infinix Note 40 has the tools to elevate your visual storytelling.

Performance-wise, the Mediatek Helio G99 Ultimate chipset, coupled with 8 GB of RAM and an additional 8 GB of virtual RAM, ensures that the Infinix Note 40 handles multitasking and demanding applications with ease. The generous 256 GB of internal storage, expandable via a dedicated memory card slot, provides ample space for all your apps, photos, videos, and files.

Battery life is another area where the Infinix Note 40 excels. The 5000 mAh battery, combined with

45W fast charging and 20W wireless charging capabilities, ensures that you stay powered up throughout the day. The reverse charging feature adds an extra layer of convenience, allowing you to share power with other devices when needed.

The Infinix Note 40 also shines in terms of connectivity and security. With features like 4G VoLTE, NFC, and an in-display fingerprint sensor, you can stay connected and secure with ease. The IP54 rating adds a level of durability, making the phone resistant to dust and splashes.

Personalization is at the heart of the XOS experience. With customizable themes, wallpapers, and ringtones, you can make the Infinix Note 40 truly your own. The unique features of XOS, such as the Folax Voice Assistant and Lightning Multi-Window, enhance productivity and user convenience, making your smartphone experience seamless and enjoyable.

The Infinix Note 40 is more than just a smartphone; it's a gateway to a world of possibilities. Whether you're capturing life's precious moments, staying productive on the go, or enjoying your favorite entertainment, this device is designed to meet your needs and exceed your expectations. Embrace the future of mobile technology with the Infinix Note 40 and experience a perfect blend of power, elegance, and functionality. Your journey with the Infinix Note 40 begins now, and the possibilities are endless.

APPENDICES

Unveiling the Specs: A Deep Dive into the Infinix Note 40

General Specifications:

- **Sim Type:** Dual Sim, GSM+GSM
- **Dual Sim:** Yes
- **Sim Size:** Nano+Nano SIM
- **Device Type:** Smartphone
- **Release Date:** March, 2024

Design:

- **Dimensions:** 74.5 x 164.1 x 7.8 mm
- **Weight:** 190 g
- **Colors:** Titan Gold, Obsidian Black

Display:

- **Type:** Color AMOLED Screen (1B Colors)

- **Touch:** Yes, 360 Hz Touch Sampling Rate

- **Size:** 6.78 inches, 1080 x 2436 pixels, 120 Hz

- **Aspect Ratio:** 20:9

- **PPI:** ~ 393 PPI

- **Screen to Body Ratio:** ~ 94%

- **Glass Type:** Corning Gorilla Glass

- **Features:** 550nit Type, 1300nit Peak, 2160Hz PWM Dimming

- **Notch:** Yes, Punch Hole

Memory:

- **RAM:** 8 GB

- **Expandable RAM:** Up to 8 GB Extra Virtual RAM

- **Storage:** 256 GB

- **Storage Type:** UFS 2.2

- **Card Slot:** Yes

Connectivity:

- **GPRS:** Yes
- **EDGE:** Yes
- **3G:** Yes
- **4G:** Yes
- **VoLTE:** Yes, Dual Stand-By
- **Wi-Fi:** Yes, with Wi-Fi hotspot
- **Wi-Fi Version:** Wi-Fi 5 (802.11 a/b/g/n/ac), Dual Band
- **Bluetooth:** Yes, A2DP, LE
- **USB:** Yes, USB-C v2.0
- **USB Features:** USB Tethering, USB on-the-go, USB Charging
- **IR Blaster:** Yes

Battery:

- **Type:** Non-Removable Battery
- **Size:** 5000 mAh, Li-Po Battery
- **Fast Charging:** Yes, 45W All Round FastCharge2.0
- **Wireless Charging:** Yes, 20W
- **Reverse Charging:** Yes

Taming The Troubles: Troubleshooting Guide For Common Issues

1. Battery Drainage:

- Check for apps consuming excessive battery in the battery usage settings.

- Adjust screen brightness and timeout settings to conserve battery.

- Close background apps that are not in use.

- Disable features like GPS, Bluetooth, and Wi-Fi when not needed.

- Ensure that the device is not overheating, as this can accelerate battery drain.

2. Connectivity Issues:

- Check if Airplane mode is enabled accidentally.

- Ensure that Wi-Fi and Bluetooth are turned on and properly configured.

- Restart the device and try reconnecting to the network.

- Update the device firmware to the latest version.

- Reset network settings to default and reconfigure Wi-Fi and Bluetooth connections.

3. **Performance Lag:**

    - Close unused apps and clear cached data to free up memory.

    - Restart the device to clear temporary files and refresh system processes.

    - Check for software updates and install any available updates.

    - Disable or uninstall resource-intensive apps that may be causing slowdowns.

- Consider performing a factory reset as a last resort if performance issues persist.

4. Camera Troubleshooting:

- Ensure that the camera lens is clean and free from smudges or debris.
- Check camera permissions to ensure that apps have access to the camera.
- Restart the device and try using the camera again.
- If the issue persists, contact customer support or visit a service center for further assistance.

5. Display Problems:

- Adjust screen brightness and color settings to optimize visibility.
- Check for physical damage or defects on the display.

- Update display drivers and firmware to the latest version.

- If the display continues to have issues, seek professional repair or replacement.

Frequently Asked Questions (FAQ)

Q: Does the Infinix Note 40 support 5G connectivity?

A: *No, the Infinix Note 40 supports 4G LTE connectivity but does not have 5G capability.*

Q: Can I expand the storage on the Infinix Note 40?

A: *Yes, the Infinix Note 40 has a dedicated memory card slot that supports expandable storage via microSD cards.*

Q: Is the battery of the Infinix Note 40 removable?

A: *No, the battery of the Infinix Note 40 is non-removable.*

Q: Does the Infinix Note 40 have waterproof or water-resistant features?

A: *The Infinix Note 40 has a splash-resistant design but is not fully waterproof or water-resistant. It is recommended to avoid prolonged exposure to water or immersion.*

Q: Does the Infinix Note 40 support fast charging?

A: *Yes, the Infinix Note 40 supports 45W All Round FastCharge2.0 for quick charging of the battery.*

Q: What operating system does the Infinix Note 40 run on?

A: *The Infinix Note 40 runs on the Android v14 operating system with XOS 14 custom UI.*

www.ingramcontent.com/pod-product-compliance
Lightning Source LLC
Chambersburg PA
CBHW071209240526
45470CB00018B/1646